CW01654841

BLUE BOAR
Chigwell
Buckhurst Hill
Loughton
Rectory Lane
167A
BUS
ABRIDGE
KLB 632

London's SUBURBAN BUSES

John A. Gray AMInstTA

LONDON
IAN ALLAN LTD

First published 1976
Reprinted 1977
ISBN 0 7110 0713 6

All rights reserved. No part of this book may be reproduced or transmitted in any form or by any means, electronic or mechanical, including photocopying, recording or by any information storage and retrieval system, without permission from the Publisher in writing.

Designed by Nicholas Lerwill

© Ian Allan 1976

Published by Ian Allan Ltd, Shepperton, Surrey, and printed in the United Kingdom by Ian Allan Printing Ltd.

By the same author
London Buses in Camera

Contents

Title page: In the far north east of the red bus area is the village of Abridge, Essex. In 1970, RT1560 could have given a very personal service to the Blue Boar's (left) patrons if they lived along the 167A route, at least./*John Burns*

This page: Transition from trolleys to Routemasters in Acton High Street in 1960.

Introduction

Following on from the popularity of *London Buses in Camera,* the opportunity is now taken to have a closer look, in all areas and senses, at the bus in suburban London, as distinct from the City, the West End and the completely rural areas.

The pattern and rate of growth of the London area is well enough known. New residential and industrial developments were encouraged by the availability of appropriate transport, which in the two decades before and one decade after World War Two, meant the motor omnibus. Much pioneering work continued to be undertaken by the London Passenger Transport Board after its inception in 1933, the ensuing period to date being covered pictorially in this book.

Main Line and Underground railways had deliberately encouraged urban development in many parts of the growing Greater London area before and during the electric tramway era. Urban Tube railway extensions, planned and started before the war and either completed or abandoned after it, helped to continue this principle. But with the advent of reliable motor bus operation, its flexibility was recognized as the economic expedient of providing public transport to, and within, newly developed areas, rather than deliberately pioneering them. Once development had been planned, bus services nearly always followed.

Competition for the bus grew from private car use especially in the 'fifties and 'sixties, and it continues, though at a slightly slower rate. This means that there are now fewer urban buses than at the peak of demand in the first ten years after the war.

This shape of urban London bus growth, partial decline and latter consolidation is meant to be reflected in the content of this book, and the collection of photographs portrays the fascinating evolution of modern road passenger transport vehicle design and operation in the urban areas of Europe's largest capital city.

Cambridge, September 1974

John A. Gray

ACKNOWLEDGEMENTS
My gratitude is offered to London Transport for its continuing help. I thank the many photographers who have supplied their hundreds of pictures; though individual acknowledgement is given at the pictures used, I especially thank these people for their many different kinds of valuable help: John Burns, James Butler, Alan B. Cross, Edward Shirras, James Whiting and Sandra, my wife.

JAG

Herald of the modern era: LTI./*Alan B. Cross*

SPECIAL SERVICE
MORDEN STN
AND
EPSOM RACE COURSE
Read
JOHN
BULL
Gentleman's Agreement
GREGORY PECK
DOROTHY McGUIRE
JOHN GARFIELD
LONDON TRANSPORT
UU 6611

In Eastern Suburbs

Top left: The first Leyland Cub operating from Barking Garage in prewar days./*J. F. Higham*

Far left: Central Area production Cubs usually had no bumper bar at the front. C92 compares with C1.

Above: Aldgate Minories in August 1949 with trolleybuses and LT 881 whose conductor rests seated on the platform step./*Alan B. Cross*

Left: Custom for Marshall-rebuilt LT1131 on the east-to-north route 236 in October 1948./*Alan B. Cross*

Right: Route 101 has always been a busy service, running through dense suburbs to the Woolwich free ferry. Leyland Titan TD18 came from United Omnibus, a London independent operator, to have only a few years' life with LPTB before the war.

Below: LTs had a long association with route 101, on which their larger than usual capacity was needed. 'Bluebird' LT1212 was about to move away from the southbound stop at East Ham town hall in August 1949./*Alan B. Cross*

Above: Trolleybus 1747 was the first of 18 AECs intended for Johannesburg in 1942-43, but came to London Transport instead. The summer's day seems to have been warm enough for all the available windows to be opened – more necessary in South Africa than in Ilford! The route number box above the rear offside between-decks is thought never to have been used in London./*Alan B. Cross*

Left: Lowbridge RLH66 going round the block at Windmill Lane, Maryland, in August 1970, to terminate at Well Street. Route 178 is now partly covered by S3./*John Burns*

Below left: The first of six Metro-Scania 66-passenger capacity standee buses at the Clapton Pond terminus of Stratford local route S2, in 1973./*Tom Maddocks*

Above: A dismal, wet Debden townscape for postwar Leyland Titan PD1 STD125./*C. Carter*

Left: East End engineering: a swing bridge on the Isle of Dogs dwarfs RT2944 in August 1973./*Tom Maddocks*

Below: RTs 1539 and 4728 about to emerge from Argyle Road, Ilford./*Edward Shirras*

Right: Route 615 was a short-lived experiment at running a one-shilling flat fare express bus service alongside route 15 between Poplar and the City. It ran for only a few months in 1970, here with Merlin MBS514 from Poplar Garage./*Tom Maddocks*

Below right: Daimler Fleetline DMS1447 with 89 passenger carrying ability MCW bodywork turns round the side streets at Canning Town on route 173, part of the formerly longer 175, so renumbered when o-m-o was introduced in 1973./*Edward Shirras*

CHARRINGTON
POPLAR
615 ST. PAUL'S STN
LONDON TRANSPORT
VLW 514G

BATTERSEA
FUN FAIR
OPEN DAILY
Newham Way
Rippleside
Dagenham Heathway
173
CANNING TOWN
BATTERSEA
FUN FAIR
OPEN DAILY
SCHREIBER
PLEASE PAY AS YOU ENTER
MLH 447L

Above: This 1949 hired AEC Q-type coach has no trailer: a 'converted T' is very close behind. In keeping with the then Metropolitan Police requirements, the door is here kept in the open position./*Alan B. Cross*

Left: The streets of terraced houses adjacent to Royal Albert Dock enabled another Leyland Titan, TD103, to turn short of North Woolwich in June 1938./*S. L. Poole*

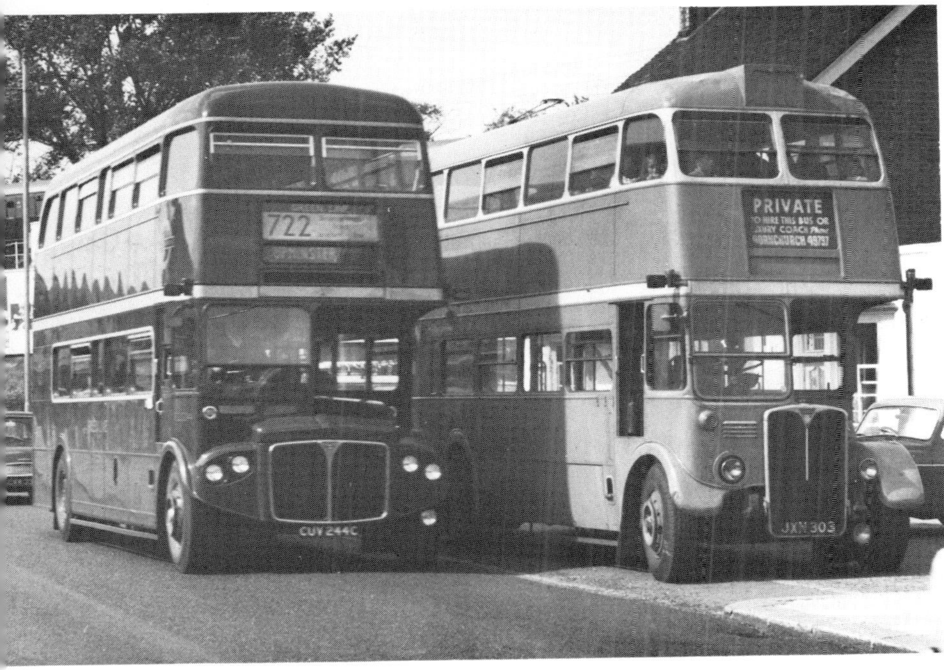

Above: Former LT RF211 had become 'RF 391' in the Super of Upminster fleet by September 1965. The numbering is thought to represent '39-seats, No 1'. The indicator, distinctly a Green Line style of the period, shows route 19 of 'Redbridge and District'. *Alan B. Cross*

Left: In nearing Upminster, RCL2244 on Green Line route 722 passes former RT925 when in Super ownership./*Alan B. Cross*

Above: Three-axle LTs for learning stand in the yard at Upton Park Garage, West Ham, in August 1949. Until the mid-1950s, buses from this garage had their fleet numbers additionally painted white on the rear roof dome for fuel recording purposes./*Alan B. Cross*

Left: Country learners still came to Chiswick Works in the heart of western suburbia for some tuition. It would have been a long haul in green ST 1076 from Grays about 25 years ago./ *S. A. Newman*

Learners

Above right: AEC side-engined Q78 on learner duty in the early 1950s, not long before withdrawal, was unusual in that drivers are seldom taught their craft on single-deckers with London Transport./*B. V. Franey*

Right: ST26 in south east London presents several idiosyncrasies. It was painted green, yet stationed at Plumstead for learner work; its L plate is not of the legal standard, and it shows no PRIVATE indication. Steering along tram-tracked streets would have given the novice bus driver a tricky job./*Alan B. Cross*

Above: Culmination of the learners' course on the old skid pan at Chiswick. STL2554's unpredictability seems to have caught the photographer by surprise, allowing a glimpse of 'prewar' RT56, ST86 and a Tilling ST./*LTE*

Below: At the end of their London life, many types are used to train drivers: RT136 from Chalk Farm Garage./ *Alan B. Cross*

Right: Leyland RTL1256 in green livery is driven by a learner along Shoreditch High Street./*Alan B. Cross*

Above right: Trolley drivers had to be trained too./*Alan B. Cross*

Far right: In the late 1960s, eight feet wide Leyland RTs became the favourites for training. RTW271. in red livery, takes a break at Aldgate after coming into town from Grays (Country Area) garage, in August 1967./*Alan B. Cross*

CROSSE & BLACKWELL
SALAD CREAM
PRIVATE
288
LONDON TRANSPORT
CUL 288

PRIVATE
To hire a bus or coach
apply 55 Broadway S.W.1
ABBEY 5600
HAVE A FLUTTER IN THE NATIONAL INTEREST
BUY PREMIUM BONDS
PINTA GIRL
LONDON TRANSPORT
KXW 371

Metroland

Above left: In the heart of the area 'opened up' by the Metropolitan Railway, with architectural styles well shown, stands Dennis Dart DA29 outside the Red Lion at Pinner in about 1932./*J. F. Higham*

Left: Rain at Rayner's Lane and two lowbridge buses on route 230 in the early 1950s: ST141 behind an STL./*James Whiting*

Above: The reason for low height double deckers on route 230 was the railway (Bakerloo and BR) bridge in Headstone Lane, Wealdstone – RLH67 demonstrates./*LTE*

Right: Route 230 converted to single-deck operation in 1969 as flat-fare route H1, with AEC Merlins such as MBS506./*Edward Shirras*

Radials

Above left: Route 3 still radiates out from the West End to Crystal Palace southwards and Camden Town northwards as it did in about 1950 when STL1766 was caught at the northern end./*F. G. Reynolds*

Left: The 7A route started here at London Bridge Station, immediately south of the City, to radiate westward to Acton High Street, on which duty ST705 was employed in about 1950./*J. H. Aston*

Above: A Routemaster's rivets are revealed on route 8./*Alan B. Cross*

Left: Route 12 was one of the longer routes so it was usually worked in two overlapping sections LT177 stands at the southernmost terminus, the Red Deer at South Croydon, in May 1948./*Alan B Cross*

Right: A prewar picture of Tilling ST839 and STL486 on route 12./*J. Bonell*

Below: Route 12 in the west this time, at East Acton, where LT349 with Cardiff Corporation-rebuilt bodywork including wind-up windows was photographed in May 1949./*Alan B. Cross*

Left: Inevitably, route 13 is portrayed with the yesteryear favourite Leyland Titan TD4 of 1937. At Golders Green in about 1953 the leader is STD68, with STD17 (red upstairs window frames) behind./*J. H. Aston*

Below: The best known east-west route is 15. East Ham has been the eastern terminus for many years now, but posed LT280 shows the one-time Dagenham blind./*LTE*

16
VICTORIA
KINGSBURY KILBURN
GY 8414

16
CR
27
LONDON TRANSPORT

Left: Some unlikely vehicles came to help the Edgware Road route 16 in 1949. Former Tilling T314 here at Victoria Station, was one./*Alan B. Cross*

Below left: This rear-engined Leyland Cub 20-seater looks to be well-filled./*Alan B. Cross*

Above: The Commercial Road route 23 was served by a 'Bluebird' with painted radiator in 1947: LT1248 at Minories./*J. H. Aston*

Right: Becontree Heath is the outer terminus of the 23, and is over-shadowed by a multistoreyed block of flats. RT4664 and RM473 in September 1969./*Edward Shirras*

Below: The other road radiating from Aldgate, Mile End Road, was served by route 25B (since renumbered 25). Another compact Cub, CR42, finds employment in the postwar travel peak./*Alan B. Cross*

Above: A route to radiate northwards from Victoria is the 29, and it had West Green Garage's 'converted' T223 assisting in August 1949./*Alan B. Cross*

Right: Advertising buses were good revenue earners by 1969 when gaudy RM686 worked on route 29./*Tom Maddocks*

Above: South east to north west double radial is route 36 and variants. Open-staircase Tilling ST852 shows a turn of speed in prewar days./*LTE*

Left: Route 38 still heads north eastwards from Victoria, though only to Leyton, not as far as Loughton when postwar STD154 was photographed on 38A.

Above: The route from Shoreditch and the City to south eastern suburbs is 47, here with former Green Line T265 giving aid, by now in Country green colours./*J. H. Aston*

Left: RT745 whose roof is almost free from any paint, caught more recently on route 47./*Tom Maddocks*

Below: Another northbound route from Victoria is the 52, on which RT1475 was working before premature withdrawal in 1956, due to its having non-standard Cravens' bodywork./*Alan B. Cross*

Above right: A fairly luxurious ride would have been given by AEC Renown private hire coach LTC16 when helping out on south-of-Thames radial route 53A in 1948./*Alan B. Cross*

Right: North to south route 59A had LT215 (with metal numerals still on its bonnet plate) working on it in prewar days. The location is Thornton Heath pond.

53A
PLUMSTEAD COMMON
OXFORD CIRCUS BLACKHEATH
BRUNTON & DAVIS
LTD
LONDON TRANSPORT
LTC16
EGO 520

ALBANY ST REGENT ST
LAMBETH BDG BRIXTON
STREATHAM NORBURY
ST JAMES'S ROAD
Daily Mail
59A
CAMDEN TOWN
LT 215
LONDON TRANSPORT
GK 5430

Above: Route 133 is another southern radial, though for about a decade from 1958 it ran on Sundays northward to Hendon. First type STL, 187, was photographed long before the extension, in July 1946./*Alan B. Cross*

Left: Two different kinds of STL on the 133 at the bombed South Croydon terminus soon after the war: 571 of the second series and 1775 of a later large batch with front route number display provision in the roof./*F. G. Reynolds*

Right: This route started as two tram replacements, 155B and 155W – Blackfriars and Westminster, according to the direction of loop travel, but was renumbered more straightforwardly by October 1951. Routemaster 1536 has the early type of body with fixed upper deck front windows in this June 1973 picture at Wimbledon./*Edward Shirras*

Below: When buses and trams gave a choice in forms of road passenger transport, STL1514 picks up at the Telford Avenue, Streatham southbound stop of route 159, a variant of 59./*F. G. Reynolds*

Complete House Furnishers
JANUS
ROUTEMASTER
LONDON'S BUS OF THE FUTURE
260
ALDWYCH
SLT 56
ROUTEMASTER
8
SHOREDITCH
JOHN COURAGE
SLT 58

26
Whetstone Finchley
Golders Green
Marble Arch
GOLDERS GREEN STN
The Sun
WORLD CUP
THIS IS AN AD FOR BUS ADS.
COURAGE
WLT 986

Above left: Two of the Edgware Road routes each sport a pre-production Routemaster! RM1 with AEC engine and LT body on route 260 which had begun in 1957 leads RM(L)3 with Leyland engine and Weymann body. The buses' front end treatments compare interestingly.

Left: Route 26 came in 1970 to take over a part of 260. RM986 comes in to turn at Golders Green./ *Edward Shirras*

Above: The Harrow Road trolleybus routes in the heyday of the C class Leylands: 325 (left) had Birmingham RCW bodywork while 276 had MCW./*Alan B. Cross*

Right: By the end of 1961 some AEC trolleys of class N2 had taken over route 662. No 1646 in front of 1657 resting at Paddington Green./*John A. Gray*

Not all Asleep

Above left: The last London Transport lowbridge bus was RLH61, caught as the passengers alight from its last service journey late on April 16, 1971 before turning into Dalston Garage. Route 178 finished simultaneously./*Tom Maddocks*

Left: Two more 'lasts' in this picture: the final double-decker on route 21A, RT2578, was photographed the last time the route terminated at Sidcup Station in October 1968./*Tom Maddocks*

A study of RML2410 and street lights at the Waterloo Bridge roundabout./*James Whiting*

N96
Stratford Plaistow
Clapton Hackney
Dalston Islington
LEYTON GREEN
THE LONDON OF CHARLES DICKENS
12/-
N96
JJD 410D

Country Urban North and West

Below left: New housing west of Rickmansworth called for the services of rebodied T362 on route 361, later largely incorporated by an extension of route 309./*F. G. Reynolds*

Bottom left: Route 309 ran through more of west Middlesex than any other Country Area route. It was served well in August 1951 by AEC side-engined Q90 with Birmingham Railway Carriage & Wagon bodywork./*John H. Meredith*

Below: In 1950, route 362B (now part of 363) traversed High Wycombe's suburbs to reach Penn village, after climbing the long hill out of the town. Early wartime STL2674 with a 60-seat body from the first STL type built eight years before the chassis descends the hill near High Wycombe station on an inward journey./*Alan B. Cross*

362B
PENN (POST OFFICE) &
HIGH WYCOMBE
By GAS that's superb!
FXT 397

ASK FOR
St Martin
CHUNKY
MARMALADE
344A WHIPPENDELL RD
WATFORD JUNC.
GARSTON L.T. GARAGE
HGC 225

Left: Watford has its own suburbs, and several groups of routes serve them. Long since discontinued is the 344A, shown by postwar STL2692 in April 1953, at the then new Garston Garage./*Alan B. Cross*

Above: Modern vehicles in Watford include Leyland Atlanteans. AN50 with a 72-seat Park Royal Vehicles body with the 1972 delivery colour scheme of Country green and yellow./*Tom Maddocks*

Right: Atlantean A N 96 has an MCW body of neater frontal appearance than the PRV style, though here in 1973 was decorated for an advertiser./*Tom Maddocks*

Above: Long Routemaster 2419 works an early journey on a Watford urban route before beginning a full day on route 347 to Hemel Hempstead in July 1970./*Edward Shirras*

Left: Residents of the Botleys Park and Holloway Hill area west of Addlestone had a more direct bus service in the 1960s. RF667 here works route 474 not long before the route's withdrawal in June 1969./*Edward Shirras*

Right: Running empty, RT3204 approaches the Weybridge works of the British Aircraft Corporation whence it will leave on route 462./*Edward Shirras*

Below: Leyland National bus LNB62 works route 303A which has the distinction of connecting suburban London (at Barnet) with three 'new' towns (Hatfield, Welwyn Garden City and Stevenage). Solving the problem of accommodating the route suffix letter when using a three-digital-separated number blind is here overcome by putting it on the left of the destination/route blind. The later solution is to re-number completely, avoiding the suffix./*Tom Maddocks*

FJJ 645

TOWN SERVICE
809
CHELLS
Good Country Beer
MAC'S No 1
Good Country Beer
TOWN SERVICE
801
LONDON TRANSPORT
HLX 414

Left: Underfloor-engined Leyland vehicles were built like TF34 before the second World War. By 1952 this former coach was working from Hertford on local routes./*F. G. Reynolds*

Below left: Stevenage town route 809 in 1969. Girls run for RT597, about to leave the Bus Station; the fleet name was coloured bright yellow, standing out more than the traditional gold./*Edward Shirras*

Above right: Stevenage has been the centre of three town bus operating schemes. First came the Blue Arrow services, introduced by London Transport on December 29, 1969, whereby employees were collected from near their homes and taken to their places of work in the morning and back in the evening. For prepaid fares, seats were reserved. Lunchtime services were operated too, but they were not so successful as the morning/evening runs. Here Daimler Fleetline XF6 speeds along Martins Way in the lunchtime of the second day of operation; from the fourth day, London Country took over the blue and silver buses./*Edward Shirras*

Centre right: Stevenage's second venture was the 'No Fuss Bus' scheme, a direct housing area to town centre o-m-o fast service to compete against private motoring. Not as successful as desired, this operation developed into the 'Superbus' idea: close frequency, cheap flat fare working, with single deckers in an eye-catching yellow and bright blue livery. Success came – so much so that Superbus outshone Blue Arrow to the extent that its vehicles took over the latter's double-deck duties, as here with SM496./*Edward Shirras*

Below: Another local Watford route was 332, here worked by red RTL850 on loan from the Central Area for a Saturday in June 1951./*Alan B. Cross*

MIDLAND BANK
LIMITED
T. WALTON — LTD
HEINZ SOUPS
BLACK & WHITE

IDLAND BANK
LIMITED
HEINZ SOUPS
ESTATE AGENTS
WRIGLEY'S

Morden

Above: Morden Station at the southern head of the Northern tube line, still looks quite new in 1934, with NSs prominent on the forecourt./*LTE*

Left: By March 1936, NSs were being supplanted by new STLs. Queues wait for buses, and buses (LT1112, ST1046, STL813) wait to leave./*LTE*

Above right: Buses still predominate the traffic scene in 1950.

Right: Busy time for Daimler D93 in May 1948./ *Alan B. Cross*

127 RAYNES PARK
NORTH CHEAM
MORDEN STN
WRIGLEY'S
NATIONAL SAVINGS
ST136
LONDON TRANSPORT
GF 7213
O.K
Sauce
PLAZA PICCA

SOUTH WIMBLEDON
127 RAYNES PARK
NORTH CHEAM
BEN TRUMAN
BEST BEER IN BOTTLE
UNDERGROUND
MORDEN
MORDEN STATION
HGC 256

Left: Morden was one of the few red bus areas in London to need lowbridge buses, whose upper deck gangways were in a trough on the offside, giving access to rows of four seats facing forward. This 1930-built ST136 featured such an arrangement. The vehicle spent nearly all its working life in the Country Area, and here at South Wimbledon waiting to return to Morden, it still wears Country green livery; 1950, a few months before withdrawal./*A.M. Wright*

Below left: London Transport's easily recognizable architectural style is exemplified in Morden Station's facade. Lowbridge Daimler D129 is pictured soon after the war, waiting to leave on the erstwhile nearly circular route 127./*P. F. Winding*

Below: Daimlers to the fore in February 1950: D101 with Brush bodywork; D197 with Park Royal; STL1655 and D81 (Duple), take on lengthy queues./ *Alan B. Cross*

Bottom: A closer look at the less austere design of Park Royal-bodied D201 in the later livery with red upper deck window frames./*F. G. Reynolds*

Above: Women climb on to ST236 on a sunny July day in 1949. The Hackbridge-Morden part of route 151 is now covered by M1./*Alan B. Cross*

Left: On its journey southward from Putney, STL609 calls in at Morden Station in July 1949./*Alan B. Cross*

Right: This Daimler, in an attractive ginger-brown and cream livery, was one of three to help in the Morden area, stationed at Sutton Garage, while on loan from Maidstone Corporation in 1949./*Alan B. Cross*

Below: An influx of passengers occurs when a Northern line train empties, and STL1813 seems to be bearing the brunt./*James Whiting*

Left: Ending its days in July 1952 on route 127, Country Area lowbridge STL1048 speeds past the camera./*Alan B. Cross*

Below: A trim utility Bedford OWB waits its departure time from the station in May 1948. London Transport had hired it from Sargents of East Grinstead, Sussex, in whose fleet it bore the intriguing number 01./*Alan B. Cross*

Right: Even on Christmas Day in 1952 there was plenty of custom for RTL1372./*Alan B. Cross*

NTH. CHEAM CHEAM
SUTTON GREEN
COLLINGWOOD ROAD
REIGATE AVENUE
ST. HELIER AVENUE
156
NTH. CHEAM QUEEN VICTORIA
Before you say PICKLES say HEINZ
156
MXX 95

Top: The station's facade had been dwarfed by a glass office block by January 1965. The buses, by now all RT family, faced the other way too./*Alan B. Cross*

Above: Single-deckers return to Morden after about a 25-year gap. Underfloor-engined AEC Regal IV RF431 waits to leave on the re-routed 80A, now one-man-operated, in March 1969./*Edward Shirras*

Above right: Many Underground stations have tower office blocks nearby, often built speculatively in the 1950-60s suburban office building boom. In March 1969, Morden's look over two Merlins, MBSs 452 and 450 on tube-feeder route M1 and RT4404 on route 151, which was later to be truncated at Sutton./*Edward Shirras*

Right: More than 100 years after Ruskin wrote about them, Carshalton's pools still lend a pleasant view to North Street. RT3581 has left bustling Morden behind on its 157 way to Crystal Palace in April 1973 and crosses the spring pools that later feed the infant Wandle./*John Burns*

MORDEN STATION
M1 Green Wrythe Lane
Middleton Road
151
VISITOR'S LOND
MORDEN STN
PAY AS YOU ENTER
PLEASE
VLW 452G
VLW 450G

157
CRYSTAL PALACE

Pay on Boarding

Far top left: Passengers paying the seated conductor as they board STL1793, with central entrance and staircase, at Haven Green, Ealing Broadway stations, in 1944./*LTE*

Far left: The 1945 pay-as-you-board STL (2284) had a separate entrance and exit, with a central staircase. Again, a seated conductor was employed. Experiments continued on the long 65 route. Running from Ealing, through Middlesex's county town of Brentford, Richmond, Kingston and Kingston's own suburbs to the country fringe at Leatherhead, the 65 gave a very fair cross section of suburban traffic conditions./*LTE*

Left: Ticket issuing machine and decorated till installed for the conductor's use in STL2284 for the 1945 experiments./*LTE*

Above: An early 1950s pay-as-you-board RF conversion. The window arrangement was not perpetuated on the Central Area PAYB buses./*LTE*

Above: The former London United Tramways' trolleybus as converted for PAYB in 1944./*LTE*

Right: Pay-the-driver RF455 at Richmond Bus Station in July 1971 on the sparsely-trafficked Great Chertsey Road route 290./ *Tom Maddocks*

Above right: Women with bags and purses at the ready, before AEC Merlin MBS466 sweeps downhill from Muswell Hill Broadway in May 1968. Buses this length, 36 feet, are considered too long for London's suburbs now that some years of operating experience have been gained. They are programmed to have a short London life for this reason./*Edward Shirras*

Below centre left: Typical inter-war housing lines the street in which Hornchurch Garage's AEC Swift SMS226 is being demonstrated with entrance doors coloured yellow, to indicate 'pay the driver'./*LTE*

Below bottom left: Merlin MB7 of the first type, once XMS, working the one-time double-decked route 108, as a one-man bus in December 1971./*Tom Maddocks*

Below: The 'Londoner' Daimler Fleetlines work as one-man-operated double-deckers on several routes, mostly in the outer suburban areas.

Suburban Countryside

Above left: Epsom, where red buses meet green, presents the air of a country town early on an October 1969 Sunday morning when green RFs 636 and 674 began one-man-operation on Country route 406A./*Edward Shirras*

Left: A deciduous setting for RF371 at Bickley, Kent, in 1970. Route 227 was one of the last two-man-crewed routes worked by RFs./*Tom Maddocks*

Above: The long 107 route has several semi-rural stretches. Rear-engined AEC Swift SM172 carries a Marshall of Cambridge body and was a standee bus (SMS) at first. The single coin-in-slot symbol had been applied in error./ *James Whiting*

Left: This Swift, SMS683, has a Metro-Cammell body of standee layout with two doors. South Mimms, where this summer 1972 picture was taken, is beyond the northern Greater London boundary./ *James Whiting*

Right: Church Cobham, now less rural than its name may imply, sets the scene for RF440 in July 1973. By then most London buses had lost their rear wheel hub covers, a decoration peculiar to many LT standard designs since the mid-thirties./*John Burns*

Below: What price the gas lamp standard now? Chislehurst was still quite 'unsuburbanised' after the war when LT1098 left for Crystal Palace./*F. G. Reynolds*

Above: Bicycle and bus – former Green Line T277 – in quiet Esher about 1948./*F. G. Reynolds*

Left: Chislehurst still has its green corners, as the background to RT1803 at the war memorial shows in October 1970./*Tom Maddocks*

Below: RM272's manoeuvre first nearly into a hedge and then backwards (*foot*) into a narrow opening is necessary when turning at Noak Hill's Pentowan terminus./*John Burns*

Right: Still in the outer north east, Lambourne Road, Lambourne End, whence RT2330 has just left, retains much bordering vegetation./*John Burns*

Left: Chessington's zoo, in Surrey countryside between Kingston's suburb Surbiton and the old town of Leatherhead, has long been an enjoyable excursion for suburban children. Square-cab ST1104, new in 1930 to East Surrey Traction Co (hence its Surrey registration mark) sets down on the way south. By 1949, its Ransomes body was looking distinctly worn./*Alan B. Cross*

110 Heston Hounslow
TWICKENHAM STN
LONDON TRANSPORT
PAY AS YOU ENTER
AML 557H

116 STAINES
Read
JOHN
HEINZ SPAGHETTI
57
LONDON TRANSPORT
T935
116
GK 1011

Garages

Above: Merlin MBS557 passes the site of the old garage at Hounslow a day or two after the type of bus was introduced there in August 1969. The new garage lies behind the bus station in the foreground./*Edward Shirras*

Left: Former Tilling ST935 leaves the old Hounslow Garage in September 1948./*Alan B. Cross*

Right: The radiator of STL565 edges into the portrait of ST475 in Sidcup Garage./*Alan B. Cross*

Right: STL1890 from Catford pauses outside South Croydon Garage./ *Alan B. Cross*

Below: In 1949, Palmers Green housed a loaned Bristol and LT920./*Alan B. Cross*

Left: Rebodied STL2477 at the stop outside its Alperton home./*Alan B. Cross*

Below: In July 1950, Alperton's yard accommodated two wartime utility Guys. G174 has the angular Massey bodywork while G95 on the right has Park Royal. The projecting painted radiators (though G95's has a polished head) allowed room behind for the six-cylinder Gardner diesel engine, though all London's utility Guys had the Gardner five-cylinder unit./*Alan B. Cross*

218 WALTON ON THAMES
PORTSMOUTH RD
LONG DITTON
ESHER HERSHAM
LONDON TRANSPORT
BXD 536
UU 6648

ACORN MOTORS L
DENNIS
AKL 472

Left: Kingston Bus Station-cum-Garage shelters Q15, a Country Area bus working on red route 215, and T33 from April showers in 1952./*Alan B. Cross*

Below left: An early 'thirties Dennis Lancet with deck-and-a-half body, hired from Acorn Motors (Acton and Hanworth) in 1948, waits to turn into Kingston Garage's back door and take up a journey on route 216. It originally worked for Auto-Pilots on its Folkestone-London service./*Alan B. Cross*

Below: At the corner of Wood Street, Kingston, with Lower Ham Road, there used to be a yard where Kingston Garage's unaccommodated buses were kept. In 1948 it had room for this hired Dennis Lancet with Wycombe bodywork which was originally Penn Bus No 26 and passed to Thames Valley in 1935 when the Penn operations were divided between that operator and London Transport. One of Ben Stanley's austerity Bedfords, also hired, stands alongside./*Alan B. Cross*

Bottom: Looking remarkably serviceable after rebuilding in 1949, LT1026 awaits allocation./*Alan B. Cross*

Right: One of Cronshaw's yellow and brown Bedford SB coaches in its own Hendon Garage with the February 1966 route stickers exhibited during temporarily-licensed operation of route 240./*Alan B. Cross*

Below: A summer Saturday afternoon in 1967 allowed many RTs to be idle in Bromley Garage./*John A. Gray*

Left: The unique FRM1 at Tottenham Garage on its first public journey, on June 26, 1967./*Capital Transport*

Below: A former Tourist Coachways' Bedford SB stands in Golden Miller's Feltham premises, into whose ownership it had passed when the Bedfont Lane route was acquired early in 1967.

Bottom: At Aldenham Works in September 1966, RF296 bears BEA's Executive Express emblems while awaiting further attention. The vehicle had started life as Country bus RF515 in 1952, was converted to a Green Line coach as RF296 in 1956, later assumed its photographed role for a short while, then reverted to Country bus operation, by one man./*Alan B. Cross*

Above: A bus on a trolley route was unusual in London, but in August 1961, Routemaster 589 ran on 609, pictured at North Finchley./*Photofive Transport*

Left: The north looked bleak in October 1948 when open staircase ST905 helped out from Potters Bar Garage on the 84 route./ *Alan B. Cross*

In Northern Suburbs

Above: The large and well-kept LCC Mill Hill housing estate features as background to Leyland Tiger TD24 at Burnt Oak./*J. H. Aston*

Left: The long 107/A route traverses many of the outer northern suburbs and has had many bus types working it over the years. This early Strachans-bodied Merlin had been a Red Arrow in central London as XMS4 before becoming MB4, here, in 1970./ *Edward Shirras*

FINSBURY PARK STN
W3 Wood Grn Alexandra Pk
Ferme Park Road
LONDON TRANSPORT
VLW 48G

CHINGFORD STATION
242 Potters Bar
LONDON TRANSPORT
PAY AS YOU ENTER
PLEASE
VLW 359G

Above left: Built as north London's leisure centre to vie with the Crystal Palace in south London, Alexandra Palace crowns Muswell Hill, as the backdrop to MBS48 on a Wood Green flat fare route./*Capital Transport*

Left: Later Merlin MB359, with a higher driving position stands before turn-of-the-century architecture at Waltham Cross; July 1969./*Edward Shirras*

Above: Chingford Station forecourt in July 1974 with RM859 and Londoner DMS433 with Park Royal bodywork./*John A. Gray*

Right: Ford Transit FS3 pulls out from Southgate Station on the residential 'stop anywhere' minibus run to Enfield./*John A. Gray*

Pubs and Inns

Above left: The forecourt of the Crown at Cricklewood served as a bus terminus for many years. In the mid-thirties, AEC London Six LS3 leaves for the haul on route 16 along the Edgware Road to Marble Arch and Victoria.

Left: The Crown in the early 'fifties had SRTs on route 16. They were stopgap buses made up from late prewar STL chassis and new RT bodies./*Alan B. Cross*

Above: One of north London's most famous inns is the Spaniards, on Hampstead Heath. The road is narrowed to little more than a bus' width by the projecting buildings, as SMS711 shows./*Capital Transport*

Left: The Harrow inn at Charlton near Sunbury is probably the only thatched hostelry in western suburbia. Golden Miller's hourly-frequency route 602 passes the door; here worked by Ford R1092 with Strachans bodywork in 1970./*John Fielder*

Right: The Bell at East Bedfont, rebuilt in a fascinatingly ornate style, gets a mention on the bus indicator, as the furthest point on the Bedfont loop of Golden Miller route 601, worked in 1971 by this Bedford VAM with Willowbrook bodywork./ *John Fielder*

Below: A famous terminus no longer: the Royal Forest Hotel at Chingford, on whose forecourt air-smoothed-styled T406 stands just over twenty years ago. The bus had been a Green Line coach, evidenced by the sideboard clips above the windows; it still was in Country green though working from Enfield (Ponders End) Garage./*S. L. Poole*

Right: 'Prewar' RT124 waits outside another Harrow inn – at Abbey Wood – on a tram replacement route in about 1952./*C. Carter*

Below: Putney Heath-bound buses turn at the Green Man: Leyland RTL1110./*J. H. Aston*

Country Urban South and East

Above left: Epsom local route 406F had a 48-seater in June 1949: ST190./*Alan B. Cross*

Left: Twenty-four years later, a single decker of 60-passenger capacity works the same route. It is swift SM 140, in National light green and white livery./*Edward Shirras*

Above: Rear-engined Leyland Cub CR13, in green livery, on another Epsom route, in 1953./*Alan B. Cross*

Right: The Croydon to Caterham short workings of route 409 passed through almost continuous urban development. This 'unfrozen' STL, 2665B, received a late body, with roof route number box removed./*Alan B. Cross*

Right: Crawley new town's routes were shared between the Country Area and Southdown Motor Services till rationalisation under the National Bus Company. Red MB379 helps out in 1969./*Edward Shirras*

Below: Coping with Saturday morning queues at Gossops Green, Crawley, is one of the first three AEC Swifts to come from South Wales Transport Company – SMW2 – in 1971. Here is one solution to the route number suffix letter problem./*Edward Shirras*

Above: Route 493 is within the Greater London Council area, yet is a London Country route, normally worked by single-deck buses (RFs) at the time of the photograph, but with the early morning journey worked by a long Routemaster coach, here RCL2236, caught at the Ramsden Estate terminus./*Edward Shirras*

Left: Before withdrawal in 1971, route 452 ran through the semi-urban areas south-east of Dartford to West Kingsdown. RF594 passes through the chalk pit area of Greenhithe on the route's last day: February 13./*Tom Maddocks*

Left: The Gravesend and Dartford area used to have more local services than it has now. Route 496A connected Rosherville with Waterdales in peak periods: RF647 was photographed soon after LCBS formation, with all reference to London Transport obliterated./ *Edward Shirras*

Below: Northfleet in July 1970 with standee Merlin MBS422 fitted with Autofare o-m-o system./ *Edward Shirras*

Above: Dartford Garage line up in March 1972 shows Swift SM517 passing RMC1479. The Swift was delivered bearing London Country insignia; the Routemaster coach has reference to previous ownership removed and the new motif on the rear offside./*Tom Maddocks*

Right: Routemaster coach 1468 on urban bus work north of the Thames estuary in August 1970./*Tom Maddocks*

Above: The corner of Lavender Hill and Queenstown Road, Clapham, where a baker's shop had been demolished by a runaway tram, in August 1950./*Alan B. Cross*

Right: LT172 is inspected after a tangle with a bollard.

Mishaps

Right: When a gas lamp had been damaged, as by LT990, there was always an explosion threat from escaping gas.

FRANKLIN.
LONDON PASSENGER TRANSPORT
55 BROADWAY
WESTMINSTER, S.W.1

Left: Still very new when this accident occurred in March 1947, Leyland Tiger PS1 TD15 was rebuilt after being embedded in this greengrocer's shop at Finsbury Park./*Graphic Photo Union*

Above: Class C1 AEC trolley 182 looks even more sorry for itself than the extent of damage would suggest.

Right: Londoner DMS1630 with a sore head at Enfield Garage in August 1974. The damage clearly reveals the double skin roof./*John A. Gray*

Below: 'They can't put my engine right, and now it takes three of them to fix a towbar while two more watch.' Green RMC1457 in trouble at Kingston Station forecourt./*Edward Shirras*

Above: Red double-deck buses of present (RM524), past (RT480) and future (DMS447) in Cecil Road, May 1973./*John Burns*

Left: Leyland Atlantean AN92 with advertisement-painted MCW bodywork in Cecil Road in August 1974./*John A. Gray*

Enfield in the Seventies

Above right: Red RT3951 leads light green and yellow AN93 at the stands for routes 217A and 310 respectively./*John A. Gray*

Right: The first Bristol buses in the Country Fleet, short LHs with Leyland engines, came in 1974. BL8, in National light green and white, typifies the newcomers, intended to take over from 20-plus-year-old RFs. The Eastern Coach Works 35-seat bodywork is about 3ft 6in shorter, but six inches wider, than the RF's./*John A. Gray*

Trans-suburban Green Line

Above left: On postwar re-instatement, routes radiating eastward from Aldgate were worked mainly by the then new Daimlers, such as D69; though TF26 was assigned to route 723, behind./*Alan B. Cross*

Left: A summertime extra in 1968 was provided by Country bus RML2349, caught here in Park Lane before entering true suburbia./*M. A. Penn*

Above: The driver of T124 leaves plenty of room for a swerving cyclist in heading for Watford in Green Line's early days.

Left: Epsom Market Place portrays a curious mixture of urban and country town building styles, acting as background to RF60, which was given a face-lift in about 1966 to more modern standards./*Edward Shirras*

Left: Though Green Line's main pattern is of crossing London radially, two later express routes are peripheral to the northern, western and some southern suburbs. Route 727, one of them, is also planned to connect three of London's airports: Luton, Heathrow and Gatwick. Here AEC Reliance RC2 picks up at Heathrow in July 1969, when its livery was the same as the modernised RFs': Lincoln green with a pale green band and yellow fleet name and motif. The RCs were to be downgraded to Country buses five years later./*Tom Maddocks*

Below: By 1973, route 727 sported a National light green and white Reliance RP2, with Park Royal coachwork of less tidy appearance than the Willowbrook-bodied RC2./ *Tom Maddocks*

Above: The south suburban connection route is 725, Windsor to Gravesend. Twenty one AEC Swifts had been ordered by South Wales Transport, but were delivered to London Country in 1972. At 36ft1in they are 2ft8in longer than London Country's Swift buses – indeed, they are slightly longer even than the more powerful Merlins. *Edward Shirras*

Right: A Green Line-type service is provided by ThamesWeald between Romford or Gravesend and Sevenoaks. Called 'Tunnel Express', the minicoach could perform a useful service connecting urban areas on either side of the Thames, now that no LTE or LCBS routes pass through the Dartford-Purfleet tunnel. The Ford Transit was photographed at Romford in August 1974./*Alan B. Cross*

In Southern Suburbs

Route 213 has meandered from Kingston to the Sutton area since 1934, though its beginnings go back 13 years further. LT1428 was the very last bus in the class, and was one of two to come from London General Country Services./ *Alan B. Cross*

Above left: Route 200 was once a Wimbledon/Raynes Park local service, before south eastward extension to Mitcham. Two children show their interest in Q154 a couple of years after the war./*P. F. Winding*

Left: Still in Green Line livery, T525 arrived at Merton Garage in 1951 to cover route 200./*Alan B. Cross*

213 SUTTON L.T. GARAGE
NORBITON
MALDEN
WORCESTER PARK CHEAM
GX 5338

Above left: Short trolleybus 86 of Class B1, a Leyland built late in 1935 with BRCW 60-seat bodywork, turns at The Green, Sutton in the early 1950s./*Alan B. Cross*

Left: Route 628 started at Clapham Junction, where Class C3 trolleybus 298 is pictured, to run through the western suburbs to Harlesden. Some of the early trolleybuses had red-painted removable metal spats partly covering the tandem wheels. The slit ventilators above 298's windscreens had been panelled over./*Alan B. Cross*

Above: Parts of south London are quite hilly, as here with RT 4090 on the approaches to Crystal Palace.

Left: At the southern edge of the vast GLC St Helier housing estate is the short-working Wrythe Green terminus of 157, where DMS633 was seen in June 1973./*Edward Shirras*

Right: London Transport's smallest buses are Ford Transits with 16-seat Strachan bodywork, whose operation is largely paid for by a GLC subsidy. B1, one of two south London routes, connects Eltham with Bromley along roads previously unserved by buses, where it can be stopped anywhere reasonable by passengers wishing to board or alight. FS11 picks up in New Eltham, in front of typical 1930s' architecture./*Tom Maddocks*

Centre right: Hackbridge, between Mitcham and Wallington, was largely built up before World War 2 though parts of Mitcham Common remain to the east of the London Road. Route 234A was extended thence in 1950, and here in 1969, RF380 keeps RT2828 company./*Edward Shirras*

Below: Old Kent Road canal bridge in December 1948 and the first numerical RTL./*Alan B. Cross*

Above: The real first RTL was No 501, pictured at Eltham about a year after delivery in 1948./*Alan B. Cross*

Left: Kingston's busy shopping centre sets the scene for a Bedford coach owned by Conway Hunt, who in February 1966, was one of several firms to take the opportunity to work some of the 40 or so routes when LT temporarily withdrew them./*Alan B. Cross*

Bad Weather

Above left: Lowbridge type STL2229, working on route 127 in a snowstorm in 1952, sets down happy travellers./*Alan B. Cross*

Left: There were particularly treacherous road conditions early in 1948. Daimler D211, then less than two years old, leaves furrows in the deep snow./*Alan B. Cross*

Above: LT1058, a 1930 AEC Renown three-axle bus, slithers to a halt in a February 1948 snowstorm./*Alan B. Cross*

Right: This short route, 262 along Sandy Lane, Cheam, to Downs Side, Cuddington, had only a few months' life. RT4280 waits in slush for absent passengers, sometime in winter 1953-54./*James Whiting*

Archway

Above left: 'Hop on a bus'. So this homegoing tube railman does just that, on Routemaster 994 negotiating Archway station's one-way street system in August 1973./*John A. Gray*

Left: One-man-operated Daimler 'Londoner' DMS395 climbs Archway Road hill, past road-widening hubbub, and machinery appropriately forming an archway – outside a store of the same name!/*John A. Gray*

Above: A girl watches RM2158 emerge into sunshine to pass Archway Tavern, where Highgate Hill begins./*John A. Gray*

Top: About to return to Archway from its Cricklewood terminus, this blue-painted Ford Transit/Strachans demonstrator was hired at the end of 1972 to ease a temporary shortage of the type./*M. Dryhurst*

Above: Seddon Midibus demonstrator returning to Archway on the cross-Hampstead minibus route C11 in 1973./*G. F. Walker*

Left: A bus procession, for once, up Highgate Hill, though the timetables do not allow for two 210s (the single-deck, AEC Merlins) and two 271s (double-deck Daimler Fleetlines) to be running at such close interval./*John A. Gray*

In Western Suburbs

Left: St Paul's Road, Brentford was the terminus of route 97, before the route's disappearance in the Ealing area flat-fare single-deck bus scheme under the early reshaping plans. STL1975 lays over in September 1953./*John A. Gray*

Above: One of the second batch of austerity Bristols, B20, at the same Brentford spot./*J. H. Aston*

Left: The Northfield Avenue bus stop, West Ealing, for southbound buses on routes 55 and 97 always gave siting problems, in order to avoid conflict with other traffic. Here, the first of the austerity Bristols picks up when the stop was at the Lido cinema's entrance. Quite often, the resiting of a London bus stop has been for the convenience of traffic other than buses, and has not met with passenger appreciation./*Alan B. Cross*

READ
Every
body
EVERY MONDAY
55
NORTHFIELDS
GREENFORD HANWELL
ADULTS ONLY
the Snake Pit
CHILDREN UNDER 16 NOT ADMITTED
WAVERLEY
LONDON TRANSPORT
D 7
HLW 86

55
Greenford Hanwell
Northfields Popes La
Acton Turnham Grn
CHISWICK STATION
BOSTON
Daily non-stop Jets
Boots
Coombe's
LONDON TRANSPORT
DRY BATTERIES
126 CLT

Left: Windmill Road, Greenford, outside the covered stall market, continues to be a terminus though buses now face the other direction. The destination shown by terminating buses is 'Greenford, Red Lion', although the public house is two hundred yards away. Postwar Leyland Titan PD1, STD157, was one of 65 bought in 1946 to ease the desperate shortage of serviceable vehicles./*J. H. Aston*

Below left: By 1968, route 55 had gained Routemasters, before conversion to an Ealing district flat fare route. RM1126 descends Greenford Broadway's hill. Till the early 1930s, this was part of the rural Ruislip Road, and then built in typical style as a new wide shopping street./*M. A. Penn*

Below: Last of the three routes to disappear in Ealing's route reshaping was 211, whose ancestry as a single-deck bus route stemmed from before LPTB's formation. AEC Regals of the T type had mostly worked it in later years; here a penultimate variant example, T754, turns from dropping passengers outside the former District line station at Ealing Broadway to stand at the Haven Green pick-up point.

Bottom: The Victorian terraced villas of Fulham Palace Road fill the view of Hanwell depot's Leyland F1 trolleybus 714, new in 1937 and photographed here during the war with white-painted front mudguards and headlamp masks./*Alan B. Cross*

KIA ORA
HOUNSLOW WEST
91
GK 3122

HEATHROW AIRPORT
81B
Cranford
Harlington Corner
PAY AS YOU ENTER
Exact fare, please
AML 43H
LONDON TRANSPORT
PAY AS YOU ENTER
Exact fare, please

Left: Blocks of flats, cyclists on their reserved track and ST415 all share the Great West Road – the prewar car-age showpiece – at Osterley in 1948./*Alan B. Cross*

Below Left: Hounslow's bus station was roofed in summer 1970. Rear-engined Swift SM43 with divided-entry single doorway Marshall body stands shaded from the August sunshine./*Tom Maddocks*

Below: Rebuilt (by Marshall) LT1168 in nearly all red livery, apart from black wings, red-oxide hubs and cream lining, picks up the queue at Feltham Hotel, en route from Hounslow in 1950./*Alan B. Cross*

Bottom: Similarly rebuilt and liveried two-axle T46 stands in Feltham Station yard as an RT mounts the station bridge./*Alan B. Cross*

Left: An independent operator, Golden Miller, runs several stage routes in the outer south west suburbs. Here in 1969 a Bristol LL5G with Eastern Coach Works 39-seat bodywork rebuilt to full-fronted style stands in Feltham Station yard waiting to leave on route 602 to Shepperton. The coach alongside was a Ford demonstrator./*John Fielder*

Below: New to Golden Miller in 1970 was the third Bristol LH chassis to be built, bodied unusually by Plaxtons with three-and-two seating at the rear to give a seated capacity of 53. The bus, referred to by its index number as no fleet numbers are used, stands outside East Bedfont church on a demonstration run when new. Route 601, Feltham and East Bedfont loop, normally traverses the Green in the other direction./*John Fielder*

Above: Entering Windmill Lane, Greenford, in July 1949: a prewar Leyland Cheetah, by now owned by Smith's of Reading, helping out on a short working of route 92, adds colour in its blue and orange livery. London Transport indicator blinds had been fitted, except for the top panel, showing 'Express' – most inappropriate! Close behind comes converted T296 helping on route 105; route 211 was its usual run./*Alan B. Cross*

Right: Leyland trolleybus 542 of class D3 faces south in Queen Caroline Street, Hammersmith Broadway, in 1948. There is a bamboo trolley-retrieval pole clipped to the standard carrying the bus stop flag; Hammersmith trolleybus depot was just around the corner./*Alan B. Cross*

KIA
fruit squash
EXPRESS
130
ORA
the fruit squa
EAST CROYDON STN
130
SALCOT CRESCENT
HEADLEY DRIVE
GRAVEL HILL
KGK 927

Croydon

Left: When buses began (on August 10, 1955) the express New Addington-Croydon link, they carried the usual 130 route number but on blue blinds, as a distinguishing mark. RT956 works the first journey, in the presence of two official-looking bystanders.

Below right: A Routemaster points the way in to West Croydon's bus station, past a prohibition and speed limit notice./*John A. Gray*

Bottom right: Atlantean XA24 takes on a passenger for the fast run to the vast New Addington residential area on the Express route C1./*James Whiting*

Right: Croydon lost its familiar route 133 in July 1971 when route 50 was extended southward to cover most of it from Streatham. One-man-operated Daimler DMS120 enters central Croydon on the first morning./*Edward Shirras*

Below: Since 1949, route 234 has linked Croydon's southern urban areas with Selsdon. By September 1971, the only rear-engined Routemaster was working on this light route. Pictured leaving the Hackbridge terminus, the bus carries an open 'bull's-eye' motif instead of the side fleet name./*Edward Shirras*

Above left: West Croydon's bus station on a sunny spring morning in 1974 with London Country's buses heading west: a Routemaster on route 408 leads Atlantean AN23 on 470./*John A. Gray*

Above: Jump – and in goes the driver, into the cab of RT3351, beginning to look its 23 years of age in 1974./ *John A. Gray*

Left: RT3185 at the bus station displays the short-lived London Country 'winged-wheel' motif./ *Edward Shirras*

Below left: Contrasts in Green Line 725: Swift coach SMA118 pulls in, Dartford-bound; RF73, here a bus but previously modernised for Green Line work, pulls out, Windsor-bound. London Country Atlantean 21 peers between them, and railings separate the woman from a Routemaster on a New Addington service./*Edward Shirras*

Above: The back of some LTs had provision for only a hand-lettered destination board: LT1189./*Alan B. Cross*

Right: Some other LTs had a normal roller blind box: LT1427./*Alan B. Cross*

Back End

Above right: Standee Merlin MBS41 in 1968 allows rear end design comparison with the LTs of nearly forty years previously./*Edward Shirras*

Right: This was the first AEC Merlin rear-end design, shown by XMB15 when at Tring in 1970. The offside grille panel and the two lift flaps give the only clues to the engine's rear location.*M. A. Penn*

Left: In November 1939, ST132 demonstrates the producer gas trailer. Gas, made in the trailer apparatus, was piped to the engine, replacing petrol as the igniting agent. Used by a few buses on suburban services, the experiment apparently caused more engine cleanliness and sluggish performance problems than could be foreseen and the vehicles were re-converted to petrol. This particular bus was one of thirteen ordered for the National Omnibus & Transport Company and had detail differences from General's STs.

Below: ST582, of the General's standard type, demonstrates well the platform arrangement. The staircase rose in one straight flight./*Alan B. Cross*

Right: On an eastern Thames-side urban Country Department route, ST1130 shows its different rear indicator arrangement from other STs. The bus was new to East Surrey Traction Co./ *Alan B. Cross*

480 GREENHITHE DARTFORD
GRAVESEND CLOCK TOWER
'ASPRO'
BEATS THE 'FLU

Above: Six lowbridge bodywork STs came from the National Omnibus & Transport Co. This urban scene shows that ST140's rear-end was more like an STL's, with handrail diagonally crossing the rear window, indicator and registration number arrangements and emergency exit top window design./*Alan B. Cross*

Left: Mounting the outside staircase of one of the first 150 LTs./*Alan B. Cross*

Above right: Leyland trolleybus 1178 of class K2 heads under the railway bridge over Putney Bridge Road, Wandsworth in postwar days when no advertisements were posted on the rear of trolleys either side of the indicators./*Alan B. Cross*

Right: London's only two axle trolleybus, AEC No 63, pictured in June 1949 from the rear shows its unusual, if not unique, four-piece indicator. A 60-seater, the bus here shows it only wants to carry one!/*Alan B. Cross*

Far right: RTC1, rebuilt from prewar RT97, demonstrates both the normal platform doorway and the emergency exit door, which was obligatory in view of the closing platform door./*Fox Photos*

628
BRISTOL
SKOL
GODFREY DAVIS

WORKMAN
AXU
189
ASPRO
SOOTHES IRRITABILITY

PRIVATE
GREEN LINE
FXT
272

Above: Part Swedish-built Metro-Scania demonstrator shows its un-London-like appearance in its first day in service on route 99 at Woolwich: January 26, 1970./*Tom Maddocks*

Right: Behind the erstwhile BEA Routemaster coaches came the trailer for carrying airline passengers' luggage between West London Air Terminal, Kensington and a London airport, here Heathrow: 1967./*John A. Gray*

Below right: Eight of these AEC Reliance coaches with Willowbrook 48-seat bodies came in 1966 for the 'Executive Express' services whereby domestic United Kingdom air passengers were carried direct from aircraft steps to the Kensington terminal./ *John A. Gray*

Above: Bagswinger ponders two long Routemasters (RML2701 is the 'tartan' liveried one) and Swift SMS671 at East Ham in June 1972./*John Burns*

Left: The squared-up rear is shown by production Metro-Scania MS4, on route S2, not SS2 as indicated./*Alan B. Cross*

Tailpiece

To a preserved future?/*Alan B. Cross*